POSITION

OF THE

PROTESTANT EPISCOPAL CHURCH

WITH REFERENCE TO

Other Protestant Denominations.

BY THE

REV. WILLIAM H. LEWIS, D. D.,

RECTOR OF THE CHURCH OF THE HOLY TRINITY, BROOKLYN.

NEW-YORK:

STANFORD & SWORDS, 137 BROADWAY.

1852.

$2 50 PER HUNDRED.

☞ *Orders for this Tract, addressed to* JOHN V. LEWIS, *Brooklyn, L. I., inclosing payment at the rate of* $3 *per hundred, will be supplied by mail, with postage prepaid, to any part of the United States.*

POSITION

OF THE

PROTESTANT EPISCOPAL CHURCH

WITH REFERENCE TO

OTHER PROTESTANT DENOMINATIONS.

BY THE

REV. WILLIAM H. LEWIS, D. D.,

RECTOR OF THE CHURCH OF THE HOLY TRINITY, BROOKLYN.

NEW-YORK:

STANFORD & SWORDS, 137 BROADWAY.

M.DCCC.LII.

Position of the Protestant Episcopal Church.

The Protestant Episcopal Church in this country, from her distinctive principles, and the place she occupies among other Protestant bodies, is greatly liable to suffer from extreme views of those within, and from unjust prejudices of those without her pale. Peculiar institutions are ever in danger of misrepresentation from friends and foes. And it is with the hope of promoting charity and unity among all who "love our Lord Jesus Christ in sincerity," that I propose to offer some brief considerations on the position of the Episcopal Church in reference to other Protestant denominations.

I. The first point of inquiry is, Whether our distinctive principles lead to the unchurching of other denominations; whether we regard any who do not retain Episcopacy, as within the visible fold of Christ, or look upon them as sharing with the heathen only the uncovenanted mercies of God?

The inquiry is needful. A bishop of our church, supposed to act as our representative in England, though not authorized so to do, is said, in the public prints, nor has it yet been publicly denied, to have made the assertion there, in a large assemblage, "that all other associations (meaning such as are not Episcopal) are not of God," putting forth the unchurching dogma in its most obnoxious form. Eminent and excellent men in other denominations, have been aggrieved by the assertion, as well as by indications of a similar character, whether that specific one be rightly or wrongly stated, which have lately been seen among us; and multitudes of churchmen have also felt themselves wronged and misrepresented thereby. It is time for us to know our true position. Was that bishop authorized in his startling proposition? Is that the doctrine of our church! This subject I would now consider.

1. Is the Episcopal Church exclusive in her claims?

We answer, first, that natural affection and Christian charity would lead us to *hope* she is not.

We are so mingled with our brethren of other names by ties of blood and friendship, in business and social relations, that there are very few of us but that have endeared friends and relatives among them. Some of us have recently left their folds, and our kindred are yet there; others were there baptized, and the graves of sainted parents are with them. We meet the members of their churches in all the pleasant intercourse of life; we admire their seeming piety; and it would go greatly against our feelings to be obliged to adopt a church system which should teach us to regard them as aliens from the covenant of promise. The tearing of one of our States from the glorious Union where we are bound together by so many links, would be but a faint emblem of such a severing of Christian brotherhood.

And, certainly, gospel charity would incline us strongly against any such exclusive doctrines. The spirit of a true Christian is, to extend hope for others as far as God's Word will possibly allow, and to err in receiving, rather than in cutting off, those who professedly belong to Christ's flock. Some, indeed, seem to find their element in exclusiveness, and to delight in the cry, "No salvation out of our pale." They need the rebuke which the Emperor Constantine gave to a harsh-judging bishop: "Set up a ladder, Acesius, and climb up to heaven by yourself." The most corrupt church deals most in anathemas, and has the largest list of heretics. True charity "believeth all things, hopeth all things," delights not to take God's strange work of judgment out of his hands, and loves to regard "all who profess and call themselves Christians," as truly within Christ's Church, unless compelled by the clearest decisions of God's Word, to judge otherwise.

2. We answer, secondly, to the question, Is the Episcopal Church exclusive in her claims? that it is to be *presumed* she is not.

Ours is a Scriptural church, and since the Scriptures give little warrant for any such exclusive dogmas, the presumption is, that they are not incorporated into our system. Allowing Episcopacy to be of divine right, and believing in apostolic succession, there is still enough in God's Word to show that, holding these, we may have a charitable hope that others who do not hold them, may yet be in the visible Church of Christ. The general scope of Scripture teaching is, that though the outward forms of divine appointment are not to be lightly set aside, they are little regarded by God himself compared with faith, charity, and holiness of heart and life. Now, since no one can deny that multitudes of our Protestant brethren are as eminent in piety as any upon earth, since we see them zealous in all the charities of the gospel, successful in reclaiming sinners, and blest with apostolic triumphs in their missions among the heathen, how dare we say, that for lacking the one outward form of Episcopacy, they are to be adjudged as out of the visible Church of Christ? God would have mercy and not sacrifice under the old dispensation, though sacrifice was his own appointment. Our Lord teaches us to judge men by their fruits, and it is observable that it is of prophets that he is there speaking; and we do certainly know that the fruits of a Brainard, or a Doddridge's labors, are good. St. Paul appeals to the results of his preaching as the signs and seals of his apostleship. Christ said, when a disciple forbade one to work miracles who followed not outwardly with the twelve, "Forbid him not, for there is no man which shall do a miracle in my name, that can lightly speak evil of me. For he that is not against us, is on our part." We well know, how our Saviour ever warmly commended piety wherever seen, above mere orthodoxy, pronouncing the faith of a Roman centurion, who does not seem to have been even a proselyte, greater than any he had seen in orthodox Israel. We know that Aquila and Priscilla, when they found Apollos teaching the way of the Lord, although he was very defective in his knowledge of the gospel, and could hardly have had any true commission from Christ, did not silence him at once, but expounded to him the way of God more perfectly, and he afterwards mightily convinced the Jews that Jesus was the Christ. We know, that when it was told Moses, that Eldad and Medad did prophesy in the camp, and he was asked to forbid them, because they did not come up to receive the outward commission, he replied, "Would God that all the Lord's people were prophets, and that the Lord would put his Spirit upon them;" and that St. Paul rejoiced that Christ was preached in any way, even in contention and strife. We know that the apostles continued to go up to the Temple, where Jewish priests officiated, long after the Jewish priesthood, which passed away at the death of Christ, had ceased to have any valid claim to be a divine institution. We know that it is a sound rule of exposition to interpret the doubtful by the plain, and therefore, though we believe Episcopacy is sanctioned by Scripture, yet as it is nowhere positively laid down as necessary to salvation, or to the existence of a church; while love for those who bear the image of Christ, is a plain duty, and while faith and holiness do clearly prove a man to be in Christ, this rule would justify us in hoping, that those who are lacking in some external points, may yet be regarded by the Saviour as within his fold. It would seem, too, that if God had designed Episcopacy to be so essential to the existence of his church, and even to salvation, he would have more clearly given that form of government in his word, even as Moses had a minute pattern of all things showed him in the Mount; and that so much of the argument in favor of our views, would not have been left to be gathered from inference and from the fathers. No one can pretend that Episcopacy is revealed in the New Testament, with any thing like the fulness or clearness with which faith, holiness and charity are set forth; why then make it of equal importance? What minister, in standing by the bedside of the dying sinner, would present the three orders of the ministry to him, as of equal moment with faith in Christ? When we add to all this, that "believing in Christ and holding the head" are ever mentioned as the great requisites of salvation; when few will go so far as to deny that multitudes of other names do believe in Christ, and will most certainly be saved; when we all allow that they belong to Christ's Spiritual Church, and that we may hope to meet them in heaven; it would seem as if we had enough to restrain us from the harsh decision that they cannot be of Christ's visible church, and to lead us to fear that our Master would not thank us for unchurching and cutting off those whom he accepts, and perhaps will exalt to thrones of glory, higher far than those of such as judge them. At least in all these considerations, and they are named as such rather than as extended arguments, we have enough to lead us to presume, that the fathers and reformers who compiled our standards, and who meant to conform them with the Scriptures, never intended to introduce into them the exclusive dogma, against which we protest.

It may perhaps be urged, that the tendency of these appeals to Scripture is to make it a matter of indifference whether we hold to Episcopacy or no. It is not so. They are thrown out as pleas for charity, and to lead us to refrain from condemning where God's Word and our own distinctive views do not require us to condemn. Should they show that any body of our Christian brethren not of our fold may be part of the Church of Christ, though defective in some particulars, it should no more lead us to think we have no advantage over them, than because we prove that a man wanting one limb may be a man, it would follow that it is no privilege to be perfect in every part. We regard Episcopacy as essential to the perfectness of a church, but not to its being, as all the limbs are to the perfectness of a man, though not to his existence.

It is further to be presumed that the Episcopal Church is not exclusive, because those who framed her standards were not so; and it is hardly to be supposed they would infuse into them a spirit which they did not feel, or teaching opposed to their known opinions and practices. The fathers and reformers of the Church of England, who had the chief hand in preparing our formularies, are well known to have been on terms of Christian fellowship with members and ministers of churches not retaining Episcopacy, to have used their aid in compiling our standards, and even in some instances to have allowed ministers not episcopally ordained, to hold livings and to officiate in the Church ot England. In the revision of the Prayer Book in this country, and the re-organization of our church, the venerated Bishop White had the principal share. His opinions with regard to the exclusive dogma are clear and decided. He says, "In connection with a determination to sustain the Episcopacy, it is not impossible that in the different grounds on which it may be rested by the different advocates of it, there may ensue a cause of disunion. We shall be safe in this matter in proportion as we continue on the ground taken by the English Reformers. They unequivocally affirmed the Apostolic origin of Episcopacy as a fact, and then, as a suitable consequence, they ordained that there should be no other ministry within their bounds. The same is the limit in our church. If any should carry the subject further, it is a private opinion, and cannot be acted upon in proceedings regulated by the canons and rubrics, without hazarding the issue intimated." And again, he says of our form of government—"There is not perceived the necessity of carrying it to the extreme of denouncing all communions destitute of Episcopacy, as departing from the essentials of Christian faith, and as aliens from the covenant of promise." It is evident from these quotations, that Bishop White did not deem it necessary to unchurch other Protestant bodies for lacking Episcopal government—that in his view the English fathers and reformers did not—and that whoever should hold such an exclusive doctrine, must hold it as a private opinion, in which he could not be sustained by rubric or canon. Is it to be supposed, then, that our standards are exclusive, when their framers and compilers were not so in their opinions? We may, indeed, have men among us who decry Cranmer, Ridley, Latimer, and Bishop White as no churchmen, but they can hardly affirm that they were fools, or so weak as to inweave into our church formularies, doctrines which they repudiated and condemned. They must allow, therefore, the presumption amounts almost to certainty, that the standards of our church are not exclusive.

3. We are now prepared, thirdly, to reply to the question, Is the Episcopal Church exclusive in her claims? Most decidedly she *is not.*

We challenge investigation of the English Prayer Book and formularies, and of our own, of our canons, and of the decisions of our ecclesiastical authorities, for one word upon this point with which a member of any Evangelical Protestant Church can find fault. There is no condemnation of his ministry, sacraments, or worship; but while every error of Rome is condemned in our articles, and while a chief characteristic of the church is opposition to Rome, there is not one word reflecting upon our Protestant brethren.

In the standards of the Church of England, there is little, if any reference to other Protestant bodies, because they were framed before those bodies, in that country, were in existence; but in our Prayer Book, remodelled while Christians of other names were all around us, so far as there is any allusion to them, there is a distinct recognition of their claims. In the preface to the Prayer Book, those of other denominations are spoken of as churches. Bishop White's well-known views enable us to determine what is meant by styling them churches, that it was not an act of mere courtesy, or a use of popular language, but an expression of doctrinal opinion. It is not to be expected that any church will settle very fully in her standard the claims of other churches. It is enough to establish her own. But as far as there is any allusion to others, it is charitable, and not exclusive. We have a right to be judged by our authorized standards, and they are remarkable for their liberality and freedom from all bigotry and intolerance.

It is a remarkable fact, too, that among all the Primates of the Church of England, with the exception of Laud, and also among all the presiding bishops of the American Church, not one can be found who has taken the obnoxious position towards our Christian brethren which some suppose we take.

But it may be asked, Though the standards are right, is not the *general feeling* of Episcopalians that of exclusiveness? We reply it is not. It is true there are some, not breathing the spirit of the reformers, who seem to rank Romanism and Dissent, as they term it, as foes equally to be dreaded, or who say that if they must choose either, they would prefer to go to Rome, and who talk arrogantly of our church as *the* church, and of other Protestants as schismatics and heretics; but they are few in comparison with the mass of our people. They are like foam on the ocean, ever uppermost and most visible, but small and empty compared with the waters beneath. They are most loud and prominent, as the worst representatives of a church usually are. And, to adopt Bishop Reynolds' metaphor, they are like the single grasshopper in the field, which will make more noise than twelve fat oxen quietly feeding. They are, in a majority of cases, such as have come into our church from other denominations, but by a sad though common process, seem most bitter and uncharitable towards the faith in which they have left parents and kindred. Never are such intolerant denunciations against our brethren of other folds heard from the lips of old churchmen, as are uttered by those who have recently joined us from the churches they anathematize. They abound chiefly in one or two of our large cities, the places, as Jefferson says, "which are like sores upon the body politic, where all the bad humors do congregate;" and, because so prominent, are supposed to express the sentiments of our whole community—which they do not. In our country parishes, though there may be three or four, who have picked up, by communication with our cities, some of the new notions of churchmanship, the mass would be startled and shocked at the idea of excluding their Protestant brethren from the pale of the church; and the preacher who should preach such a doctrine to them, would be requested to let other denominations alone. The general feeling in cities and in the country is not that of bigoted exclusiveness.

But we may go one step further, and assert, that our church has in a measure, recognized other Evangelical Protestant bodies, as a part of the visible and true Church of Christ. We receive their communicants in all our churches to our communion, without examination, or certificate, or rebaptizing, which is more than some of them do among themselves. And moreover, we allow their baptism. No minister among us has positively refused to admit its validity, though some ultraists are very happy to rebaptize. No bishop has ever hesitated to confirm those baptized in other denominations, and of course if there were no baptism, there could be no confirmation. And baptism makes us members of the visible church, for we are therein, as our Catechism says, made members of Christ, children of God, and inheritors of the kingdom of heaven. Hence it follows, that all the baptized in other folds, are members of Christ's visible church. It makes no difference in the argument, whether we say their ministry is a ministry, though defective, or their baptism is no better than lay-baptism; either way their people are baptized—that is a ruled question; and they are, therefore, as much members of the church, so far forth, as we are. It was proposed in our General Convention, some years ago, to pronounce the baptism of other denominations invalid; but this was rejected by a large majority. How dare any, then, exclude from the Church of Christ those who have been baptized into His body—not only with the outward washing, but in many cases also with the regeneration of the Holy Spirit? Indeed, a bishop of our church, of as high standing as any other, has been understood to say, that unless we admit other denominations to be a part of the Church of Christ, we overthrow our own church, because many of our archbishops and bishops were baptized in churches non-Episcopal; and if they were not truly baptized, they were not in the church, and if not themselves in the church, of course all their ordinations and other acts have been invalid. However this may be, we allow their baptism, and by consequence allow that they are a part of Christ's visible church, as we are sure that they are also, in many cases, of that church which is spiritual and invisible.

Again, we may observe, that ultra-churchmen have no difficulty in recognizing the Church of Rome as a church, because she retains Episcopacy, though corrupt in almost every other point, but cannot receive Protestant bodies as churches, because they are defective in the one point of Episcopacy, though right in nearly every other. Now the question is, which would most invalidate a claim to be a Church of God—all the abominable idolatries and corruptions of Rome, or the one defect of a want of Episcopacy? Which would our Lord judge to have the best title to that name: those who worship Mary, blaspheme God, seal up His Word, and deluge the earth with the blood of His saints, but withal have the three orders in the ministry; or those who have a valid baptism, an open Bible, soundness of faith on all vital doctrines, holy living, and primitive zeal and success in missions, but have not the three orders of the ministry? They can know but little of Christ, who can doubt for a moment that He would find His home and Church among our Protestant brethren, and worship with them, if now upon earth, rather than among the splendid abominations of Popery. And yet some of our periodicals, in their statistics of churches, give those of Rome; but pass over all Protestants out of our pale, as not worthy of the name of churches.

We may remark further, that there are some things in our church that give us an appearance of exclusiveness, which has no reality. Our forms of prayer would hinder ministerial exchanges, if there were no other reason, for ministers of other denominations hardly could, if they would, conduct our worship; and there could be no exchange but by making both churches Presbyterian or Methodist in their mode of worship for the day, which would be an unequal bargain;—although this is a difficulty not insuperable. But, our conscientious views of the ministry oblige us to receive none in *our own church* except such as have been Episcopally ordained. We judge not the ministry of others, but for ourselves we can receive none but such as are called in what we deem the divinely appointed way. There is no uncharitableness in such a maintenance of our own views.

A few quotations from some of our divines, in addition to those from Bishop White, may be given, in confirmation of the positions now advanced. Bishop Andrews says, "Though Episcopal government be of Divine institution, yet it is not so absolutely necessary as that there can be no church, nor sacraments, nor salvation without it. He is blind that sees not many churches flourishing without it." Archbishop Wake says, "Far from me be such an obdurate heart, as that, because of this defect, (i. e. of Episcopacy,) I should say to some that they are to be cut off from our communion, or that I should pronounce, with over-ardent writers among us, that they have no valid sacraments, and are scarcely Christian." Hooker, one of the greatest names among us, allowed the churches on the continent to be churches, although he deplored their lack of Episcopacy. Bishop Burnet, some of whose writings are made text-books in our General Seminary, says, "A man might lawfully communicate with a church that he thought had a worship and a doctrine uncorrupted, and yet communicate more frequently, with a church that he thought more perfect. I myself," said he, "had communicated with the churches of Geneva and Holland, and yet at the same time communicated with the Church of England." Quotations of a similar character from our standard writers, such as Cranmer, Jewell, Whitgift, Hall, Tillotson, and Porteus, might be multiplied, but enough have been given to show, that the view I have endeavored to maintain, that Episcopacy is essential to the order and perfectness, not to the being of a church, and that our church is not exclusive in her claims, is that of our formularies, and of our best divines. No church on earth is more liberal in its standards, nor are the members of any church, taken as a body, more free from bigotry and intolerance, than our own. Our constant prayers are offered "for God's holy church universal, that all who profess and call themselves Christians, not those merely whom we call so, "may be led into the way of truth, and hold the faith in unity of spirit, in the bond of peace, and in righteousness of life."

II. We now go on to the second point, viz., the comparative influence of the Episcopal Church in furthering holiness of heart and life.

Our Protestant brethren, with the admission that there are many excellent men among us, are very apt to insinuate that we are, upon the whole, compared with other Protestant churches, greatly wanting in piety. Their habitual mode of speaking of us, is, "Oh there are and have been some good Christians among Episcopalians, such as Milnor," and one or two others that perhaps they may name, as if, when they had named these, they had named all, and as if these were exceptions to the general rule. But they assert that, taken as a body, there is very little vital godliness among us; that the Episcopal Church is a church for gentlemen,—a fashionable church,—a church in which there are no revivals, no conversions, no belief in a change of heart, with other slurs of a kindred character. They blame us for exclusiveness, because we consider them defective in the outward form of the ministry; did it never occur to them, that there was as much exclusiveness in denying us the inward spirit of religion? The most ultra churchman says nothing against the personal piety of our Protestant brethren, but they make no scruple in denying its existence among us. There is such a character as an Evangelical, as well as a formal Pharisee, and it seems to us at times, as if we beheld him, standing and praying thus, with himself: "God, I thank thee that I am not as other men are; formalists, semi-papists, using crutches in prayer, or even as these Episcopalians; I keep no fasts or saints-days, I believe in experimental religion and a change of heart, and I give largely of all I possess to Bible and Tract Societies, and the great Evangelical institutions of the day." God forbid that we should make any sweeping accusation of Pharisaism against our brethren as a body; but it is fair to show them that there are two sides to the picture, and how their exclusiveness strikes us, as they show us how our exclusiveness appears to them.

Whether there be, comparatively, a low standard of piety among us, God alone can truly judge.* "We have none to boast of," was the remark of Bishop Griswold, when told that there was little vital religion among Episcopalians. We know not, however, why there should not be true godliness among us. We have more of the reading of Scripture in our churches than in any other; our Liturgy is devout enough for the holiest saint, all the doctrines of grace are clearly held by us. The need of a new birth unto righteousness, is a prominent article. And as to the preaching of Christ crucified, it has been repeatedly acknowledged by visitors from other churches, that they heard more of it in our pulpits than in their own. Whether this be so or not, we will not dispute, but this we may say, that our Liturgy compels us every year to follow Christ in all his work and offices, from his incarnation, to his death, resurrection, ascension, and gift of the Holy Spirit; and it is usual for our clergy to adapt their preaching to the services, so that we may be less likely to wander off to abolitionism and other semi-secular subjects of the day, in the pulpit, than others. We might appeal again to the fact, that so large a portion of the standard theological works in every library and in every closet of devotion, were written by Episcopalians, as proof that our system is not unfavorable to piety. We might appeal to the names of Hall and Leighton, Richmond and Martyn, Scott and Newton, with a host besides, and ask, if they found room enough for such attainments

* Dr. Baird, in his learned work entitled, "Religion in America," in speaking of the sad consequences of the war of the Revolution upon the Episcopal Church in Virginia, holds this remarkable language in reference to the present condition of the same church:

"I do not think it possible to find a body of ministers of equal number, in any denomination, who, in point of theological education, prudent zeal, simple and effective eloquence, general usefulness, and the esteem in which they are held by the people, can be regarded as superior to the Episcopal clergy of the present day in Virginia." p. 114.

The same learned author, in speaking of the church generally in reference to her recovery from the ruinous effects of the war of the Revolution, remarks: "Nor has the spiritual prosperity of the church been less remarkable than its external. It possesses a degree of life and energy throughout all its extent, and an amount of vital piety in its ministers and members such as it never had in its colonial days. It is blessed with precious revivals, and flourishes like a tree planted by the rivers of waters"——"The prospects of the Episcopal Church in the United States are certainly very encouraging. The friend of a learned and able ministry, to form which she has founded colleges and theological institutions, she sees, among her clergy, not a few men, of the highest distinction for talents, for learning, for eloquence, and for piety and zeal." pp. 222, 223.

in holiness in our church, whether it can be possible that its natural tendency is to blight and dwarf the plants of grace, in the believer's soul. The holiest of them would testify, that as the result of his own experience, he could conceive of nothing better adapted to further experimental godliness, than our Liturgy. If there be not among us all that can be found elsewhere to promote the great work of conversion and sanctification, we should say of our church, with its bitterest foes, "Raze it, raze it even to the ground."

As to scandals, from the sad lapse of ministers and members, we shall, on neither side, be over-ready to cast the first stone; knowing that each has enough such cases to bow our heads in shame. We believe, however, that we have the most effective discipline for the erring, strong enough to take the mitre from the most powerful bishop when he offends, as well as to correct the humbler backslider; and prompt to act, without any long vexatious delays.

III. A third point of consideration, is, the efficiency of the Episcopal Church in the missionary work compared with that of other Protestant churches.

We are told that "we are doing comparatively very little, in the Foreign or Domestic field."* We acknowledge our deficiencies; yet there are some things to be taken into consideration, which will show that they are not so much the defects of our system, as of accidental circumstances. It will be acknowledged that the strength of our brethren, in their missionary operations, lies in New England, and among the descendants of the Puritans. And it is also well known, that Puritan bigotry and intolerance persecuted, and drove out Episcopalians from New England, and that the results of the Revolutionary War were further disastrous to the interests of our church there, so that the rich mine for benevolent operations in that region has been kept, and worked almost exclusively by our brethren. Our churches have been few and feeble, overtopped and shaded by that which was, for a long time, in point of fact, the established church. We are now gaining ground there very rapidly, insomuch that our growth under

* Dr. Baird, in his able work entitled, "Religion in America," published in 1844, shows that the contributions of the Episcopal Church in the United States to Foreign Missions, in proportion to the number of her communicants, were as compared with other churches, setting aside decimals, as follows:

As compared with the Presbyterian, as one dollar and twenty cents to one dollar; as compared with the Methodist, as ten dollars to one; as compared with all others together, as two dollars to one.

these unfavorable auspices, is a matter of astonishment to ourselves. And we think that when our church, which in all parts of the country has hitherto been struggling for its very existence, and recovering from the effects of the Revolutionary contest, shall have gained a footing, she will take her place among the foremost in the missionary work. We have been retarded also by defects in our missionary organization, which it is not necessary to explain, but which have kept back the wealth and zeal of multitudes, or turned them into other channels. We are doing something, however, and it may be named, that in the deadliest climate in the world—in Africa, we have two missionaries to one from any other Protestant denomination. That there is nothing unfavorable to missions in our system, may be seen in the mother country, where Episcopalians have been as early, and as earnestly in the field, as any of their brethren. The oldest Protestant Missionary Society in the world had its origin with churchmen.

And the first religious service and administration of the Lord's Supper by a Protestant, or perhaps by any other, in North America, nearly one hundred years before the landing of the Pilgrims, was by an Episcopal minister; the first Protestant church in the limits of what is now the United States, was Episcopal, and the first service in New England was by an Episcopal minister. We hope, that we who were the first to take possession of the country, in the name of the King of kings, may be found doing our part in retaining it for him, as well as in setting up his kingdom throughout the world.

IV. A fourth point of consideration is, our position compared with other Protestant churches in regard to patriotism.

The old charge that in the Revolution, many of our clergy and people were tories, taking the part of England against the cause of liberty, is often urged against us; and it is asserted "that Episcopalians have never been pre-eminent in patriotic exertions for the welfare of our glorious country." This is a charge, which among vulgar railers answers a very good purpose in exciting popular prejudice, but ought never to be advanced by the intelligent Christian opponent. We furnished a Washington for the Revolutionary struggle, but we did not, so far as I have ever heard, furnish an Arnold. Nor was it the characteristic of churchmen to *fight against* their country, but rather to remain passive in a war which some of them did not approve, or else to withdraw to England or the Provinces. The first prayer offered in Congress was by an Episcopalian, which shows that the feeling then among intelligent patriots, could not have been very hostile towards us. We allow that there were some of our church who took sides with England, more perhaps than of any other denomination; but they were generally conscientious men, who did not see how they could be released from their oath of allegiance—a subject which has troubled other consciences in similar cases—and whose after sufferings testified to their sincerity. There is that in the Episcopal Church which makes her members not easily given to change, and the same principle which led some of them to hold on, then, and to sustain the dominion of the old country, may hereafter lead others to cling to, and sustain republican institutions, when some of our Protestant brethren may have become supporters of despotism. We claim for our church that she is more truly republican than any other in her mode of government, her legislation, and her happy union of popular will with conservative checks.

Some allowance also should be made for the conduct of a few of our church in the Revolutionary struggle, from another consideration. It is natural for men to take the part of those who show them most sympathy. If a despot should now make war upon our liberties, it is not at all unlikely that the oppressed would side with him, rather than with the upholders of republicanism; not because it would be right, but because they had never met with kind treatment from the friends of liberty. Now, the Episcopal Church, before the Revolution, was harshly treated by other denominations. It amazes us in these days of toleration to read of persecution, fines, and imprisonment endured by members of our church, merely for seeking "freedom to worship God," from those who professedly fled to this country to gain the same privilege. We blame not the Puritans. Intolerance was the fault of the age. Whoever had the power, whether Churchmen or Puritans, exercised it in persecuting supposed errorists, and thought they were doing God service. But how natural it was that Churchmen, ground down by such bigotry, should sympathize with Churchmen in England rather than with Puritans at home. Had they been treated with tolerance, the very men who left us might have been as patriotic as any others in the Revolutionary struggle. We do not urge this to justify their course, but only to show that there were faults on both sides which led to it.

That there is nothing in our church unfriendly to republicanism may be proved by recalling a few distinguished names, against which patriotism will offer no exceptions. Washington and Jay, of our church, among Revolutionary scenes,—Washington, Madison, Monroe, Harrison, Tyler, and Taylor, who were Episcopalians, as Presidents,—Taylor and Scott, as soldiers,—Webster and Clay, as statesmen, both of whom made their sacramental profession of religion, it is believed, in the Episcopal Church; the latter his only profession, and the former his first after years of neglect,—Marshall and Kent, among jurists,—Irving, and Sigourney, and Cooper, among popular writers,—are names that have reflected honor upon our land, and enough, considering how small our numbers have been, compared with those of other churches, to wipe off the slander that "we have done nothing for the welfare of our glorious country."* Some of these were late adherents of the Episcopal Church; but their testimony is none the less strong, for it proves that in their matured judgment there was nothing in Episcopacy conflicting with patriotism, or unfavorable to piety. Great names in the political world are not indeed usually worth much in the kingdom of Christ. We give these because they are worth as much as any other, and to repel an aspersion.

It should be observed further, that until very recently, all the leading schools and colleges of our country have been under the control of our Protestant brethren. The Earl of Dartmouth and Bishop Berkeley were early and liberal friends of our learned institutions; of whose liberality, however, those out of our pale have enjoyed the chief benefit. We have now colleges of our own, which are rising into notice, and will hereafter, we trust, add our quota of men prominent in our literature and political affairs.

* At the period of the Revolution a very large proportion of the Episcopal clergy were Englishmen by birth, and connected by strong ties of duty and interest to the mother church, and in many cases dependent on her for support. It is not strange, therefore, that the war should have caused a majority of the Episcopal clergy to return to the land of their birth, and that this state of things should have caused great suffering to the church. On this subject Dr. Baird remarks: "This was no doubt counteracted so far by there being in the minority of the clergy such staunch republicans and avowed partisans of the colonies as the Rev. Dr. Madison, afterwards bishop of the state; Drs. Griffith and Brachen; Messrs. Buchanan, Jarratt, and others. While, as regards the laity, no men in all the colonies entered more warmly into the Revolution than did the Episcopalians of Virginia." p. 113.

Among the distinguished laity of the Episcopal Church of Virginia during the Revolution, may be named Washington, Patrick Henry, the two Lees, Mason, Pendleton, Lyons, Carrington, Fleming, Grayson, the Nelsons, Meades, Mercers, Harrisons, Randolphs, and hundreds of other names dear to Virginia. The same remarks will hold true in relation to the character of the church at that time in other States.

V. The next point is, our comparative position as an opponent of Rome.

It has been asserted, that "where the Episcopal Church makes one convert from Rome, other Protestant churches make ten, if not ten times ten;" and it is often brought against us as a reproach, that "numbers have gone over from our church to the errors of Popery." This will lead us to consider the comparative advantages of our system and theirs, as an antagonist of that common enemy.

We appeal first to the facts that all England, the home of their ancestry and ours, was converted from Rome by Episcopalians—that the English Reformation was won and sealed with the labors and blood of Episcopal bishops and martyrs alone—and that almost the only countries where pure Protestantism prevails, received their religious inheritance of a reformed faith through our church. Surely our brethren should not speak slightingly of Episcopacy as an antagonist of Popery, when under her banners the first great victory, and that which has made all other victories easy and bloodless, was gained. We appeal to history, from the days of the Armada, when Popery rose in wrath against one church of England Queen, down to the days of Pius IX. and Cardinal Wiseman, when its efforts were renewed against another church of England Queen, to show that Rome has ever regarded that church as the great bulwark of Protestantism. We appeal to what is now going on in Ireland, where a single diocese, with a bishop and clergy as evangelical as any in the world, numbers its converts from Popery by tens of thousands, to disprove the assertion that where we make one convert other Protestants make ten, or ten times ten—for where can they point to like success? We appeal to our thirty-nine articles, more than half of them protesting against the errors of Rome. And we might also tell of successes in the warfare with her in this country. We are not in the habit of publishing the names and all the circumstances of the conversion of Romanists, as is done by colporteurs and others. We doubt the expediency of it, as much as we should of the physician's giving the details of every cure in every private family to the public. But we can assure our brethren, that every minister of any experience among us knows what it is to meet with converts from Popery, and to number them among our communicants, and that not a few of us have had the satisfaction of aiding Romish priests to enter upon our own ministry. We can assure them also, that multitudes in leaving the corruptions of Popery, find in our church a more congenial home than among those, who, in their abhorrence of Rome, have gone to the other extreme of bareness and baldness in the worship of God. Our church compared with other churches has been, is, and is best fitted to be the successful antagonist of Rome.

But we are accused of having had many perverts to Rome from our ranks. True, the army nearest the conflict will suffer most by desertion, as we have seen that ours also has by bloodshed in the actual battle. We regard that which is now witnessed in the world as the last struggle of the beast, and expect to suffer. We expect that in this sifting season, when God calls his people to come out of Babylon, and they obey by thousands, that a few hundred may go in and be partakers of her plagues. Such is the law of affinities in the kingdom of Christ.

But further: in a large majority of cases, those who have gone over from us to Rome, have been educated among our Protestant brethren. We think there is something in their system which unsettled these perverts, and prepared them for change. We are sure that there is nothing in our church calculated to unsettle. Rarely indeed does one educated among us leave his faith. The fixedness of the liturgy imparts itself to those who worship with it. This is proved by the fact that only one Episcopal church, and that not truly an exception, ever went over in this country, or in England, to Unitarianism, while lapses of this character may be reckoned among our brethren by hundreds. The same remark is true with reference to Universalism and the sect called Christians. Our church has not been their reservoir. Our people are not given to change. Such a thing as a pervert to Popery, twenty years ago, would have electrified our whole community. But there was a day when our church began to stand very high among our brethren in this country. They looked towards it as a peaceful home. They flocked into it by hundreds and thousands. Prosperity elated us, and we needed a chastisement. Those who came among us were prepared by their previous education for further change, and passed on to Rome after doing us immense injury. And so we account for many of these perversions. And thus we received our chastisement—a chastisement which leads us to sigh for the days when our accessions were smaller, innovations in our services fewer, and perverts almost unknown. This, we say to aged ministers and Christians of other churches now agonizing over sons who have passed through ours to officiate at

Romish altars, or remain in ours to raise semi-papal altars,—this is our version of the matter. We accuse your system as partly in fault. We point to the known principle, that minds once unsettled are apt to change often, and to go to extremes. We feel that the last great battle with Popery is going on, and expect to suffer as the foremost ever do. We acknowledge our need of chastening for pride and vainglory; but we do not allow that our church is comparatively a feebler antagonist of Rome than yours.

We have thus taken up and considered in several points of view our position as Episcopalians, in reference to other Protestant churches. It will be seen that the argument has been put forth in self-defence. And now in conclusion, it will also be seen that there has been much that is wrong on both sides, and that both have much to learn in the way of charity and forbearance. And so it has ever been in the contest between us and our Protestant brethren. If they suffered from Laud and the Stuarts, several thousand ministers of the church of England ejected from their livings, testify that they could inflict suffering, when in power. If they fled from England to find religious liberty, their treatment of Episcopalians and Quakers shows that they could not grant it to others. If they declaimed against the deadness and formalism of the English clergy, they sunk down at one time in favored New England, into a state as dead and formal. If they have well-founded complaints against us now, we have also against them. Would it not be most desirable if all these errors of the past could be forgiven and forgotten, and the mutual recriminations built upon them could cease, and that better time arrive, when "Ephraim shall not envy Judah, and Judah shall not vex Ephraim?" If that period shall ever come when all shall be one in Christ, a day for which our Lord and every true follower of his prays—a day which must come before the millennial glory shall begin, its advent will be heralded by a disposition among Christians to see how nearly they can agree, rather than how many grounds of disagreement they can find; how much there is in each other's systems to love and hold in common, rather than how much to censure and separate upon. And to further that spirit, let us by way of inference from all that has been advanced, notice finally, what we have a right to expect from our Protestant brethren, and then what we owe to them, and to ourselves in reference to them.

1. We have a right to expect that they should candidly consider our views of the ministry.

They blame us for our exclusiveness and grieve at our position; why do they not help us out of it, when they can do it without any sacrifice of conscience? We conscientiously believe in Episcopal ordination. They all allow its validity. Why then, if they love peace, and dêsire unity so much, do they not receive Episcopal ordination? They can do it without any sacrifice of conscience. We cannot yield without the sacrifice; and if ever the church is to be united, it must be by concessions in things not held as matters of conscience. Suppose they are not fully prepared to receive Episcopacy as of divine right, as many members of our own church and more of the English church are not, still, why do they not say, we will yield up this point to the scruples or the weaknesses, if they please, of our Episcopal brethren—we have no objection against their ministry, therefore, for the sake of that unity which all ought to desire and which Christ enjoins, we will be Episcopally ordained.* To talk of a love of union, and to lash us for our exclusive position while we cannot get out of it, and they, with no violence to conscience, can help us out, seems unreasonable. We prize our Liturgy, but none of us hold to it as of divine right, and therefore if all churches were Episcopal in their ordination, we could easily unite with our brethren, though some might retain a worship without forms. It is the ministry which proves the great cause of separation. It is well known that many a distinguished aged minister among them has said, that if he were to live his life over again he would enter the Episcopal ministry; that many have actually made the change; and that there are few prominent men among them, but that have at times had serious thoughts of such a step. While then there is so much in our claims as to stagger the minds of some of their ablest men and learned professors, have we not a right to expect as a matter of concession, if not of conviction, that they should take this great, and perhaps only bar of union out of the way? We do not ask our brethren, if they come among us, to adopt the errors of our ultraists, but rather to help repress them; but we do ask whether, with a moderate Episcopacy, they can find aught in our church to justify their longer separation from us. How desirable, even to them, in the work of missions among the corrupt churches of the old world which yet retain Episcopacy, would it be to go among them with an Episcopal form of government! How de-

* The argument for Episcopacy would be foreign to the purpose of this Tract. It may be found in our Standard Divines, and especially in Bishop Onderdonk's "Episcopacy tested by Scripture," in connection with Dr. Barnes's reply.

sirable such union for the honor of our common Christianity and Protestantism, now the scoff of Infidel and Papist because of our dissensions—for the success of the Gospel among the heathen, for our own comfort, and for the glory of our Lord! At the first hearty movement towards such union, Satan would leap affrighted from his throne, and "great voices would be heard in heaven, saying! The kingdoms of this world are become the kingdoms of our Lord and of his Christ, and he shall reign for ever and ever."

To those who *do* come among us from other folds, we say, beware of going to extremes. We have suffered so much from the over-strained zeal of proselytes, that we would ever urge this caution. You will find a home among us, a Liturgy, a doctrine, a ministry, that will fully satisfy you, and the more perfectly the more you know them; but do not magnify, out of all proportion, what is true, because it is new to you,—be moderate churchmen,—remember that piety of heart is the same in all churches, and justify your choice of ours by increased holiness.

Or if any cannot conscientiously unite with us, let us ask their forbearance. They may not fully understand us. We may be doing God's work. We may have more of vital godliness amid our forms than they suppose. "Let us not, therefore, judge one another any more, but judge this rather, that no man put a stumbling-block or an occasion to fall in his brother's way."

2. And finally, we, as Episcopalians, have also need of greater charity. No wonder that our brethren of other churches have become soured towards us, when they have been assailed by misguided zealots and bigots in such terms as I have quoted. There is no warrant, as has been shown, for denouncing them as "heretics and schismatics," or as "communities not of God." They who have done so have gone beyond our standards and standard divines. Modesty and humility should have taught them a better lesson. And it becomes all who love our church to rebuke such a spirit, and the utterance of such sentiments. Let the laity set their faces against arrogant claims and exclusiveness in bishops, presbyters, and, where it is more commonly found, in unfledged deacons. We have reason to recall again and again the counsel of Bishop White, that we shall be safe so long as we keep upon the moderate ground taken by the English Reformers. It is a poor way to expect to make converts to our church by assailing others. Our best evidence of apostolic character will be found in apostolic holiness, labors, and success. As a general rule, it will be seen that those ministers who are ever harping upon our claims,

and are most arrogant in urging our distinctive principles, are men who do us little credit by their piety, and are best known by their success in running down and destroying the churches where they may officiate. They seek to make up in boasting of externals, what they lack in the internal spirit of religion, as the Jews cried, "the temple of the Lord are these," to cover their want of piety.

But on the other hand, we are not called upon, while liberal and tolerant to other denominations, to give up our own distinctive principles. We need not imitate the examples of some ultra low Churchmen, who seem to court popular favor by ever declaiming, before those of other denominations, against the corruptions of their own church,—seeming, like children, to find every thing better elsewhere, than what they get at home, and in heart more Presbyterians or Methodists than true Churchmen. Such men should either leave us, as some to our relief have done, or be more in spirit with us. If we *have* the evils against which they declaim, we ask them where can they go that they will not find evils as great? We are in a strong position; let us maintain it, without intolerance towards our brethren, and without lowering those claims which we believe to be of scriptural authority. We are in a church that offers all that we need for personal holiness, or for the advancement of Christ's cause. Let us hold our principles with firmness, and yet with charity, and let us seek to carry out the mission of our beloved church on earth, by a purity and zeal corresponding with the high pretensions we make for her, as primitive and apostolic in her ministry, devout in her worship, and scriptural in all her doctrines. Could we stand upon that moderate ground which the fathers and reformers intended we should occupy,—could we cease to vaunt our claims in words, and establish them rather by our holiness and by our success in turning sinners to Christ,—could we stand before the world, commended to the love of all by eminence in piety equal to our soundness of faith, and the primitiveness of our ministry and worship,—we should scarcely need any other argument in favor of our church, and all around would say, "We will go with you, for God is with you of a truth."

THE END.

STANFORD & SWORDS,

NO. 137 BROADWAY, NEW-YORK,

Have in press, and will shortly publish, a second edition of Sermons fo[r] Christian Year, by the Rev. Wm. H. Lewis, D. D., 445 pp., octavo, conta[in]ing a Discourse for every Sunday and principal holiday throughout the ye[ar,] designed for Lay Reading and family use. Price $1 25.

The Right Rev. Carlton Chase, D. D., Bishop of New Hampshire, whom, as acting Diocesan, at the publication of the first edition, the volu[me] was submitted for approval for Lay Reading, says of the Sermons, i[n a] letter received from him, "They are precisely such compositions as I [can] with pleasure and confidence place in the hands of Lay Readers in our [va]cant parishes. For such a purpose I can truly say I know of nothing bett[er."]

The following brief extracts from notices of the volume in our variou[s pa]pers and reviews are also added:

"The merits of the volume we cheerfully acknowledge. It is, throu[gh]out, an earnest, cogent, clear exhibition of practical Christianity. It d[oes] not avoid doctrinal statements, which are often very distinctly made, a[nd] happily illustrated, but still its main scope is practical. For reading in [va]cant parishes or in families, this volume has claims beyond most that we h[ave] seen. The discourses are short, simple, clear, and earnest. And the wh[ole] tone of the book is Churchly and loyal.—*Calendar.*

They are plain and practical, calculated to be useful to the souls of m[en.] They breathe the spirit of a minister anxious to promote the best inter[ests] of those who hear him, and will be found a valuable aid to lay read[ers,] heads of families, or to travellers by land or sea."—*[Episc]opal Recorder.*

"Written in a plain, earnest style, such as might be expected fro[m a] zealous pastor of twenty-five years' experience."—*Jour. of Commerce.*

"We have read a number of the Discourses in this volume with m[uch] edification. The style of Dr. Lewis is plain, direct, and forcible, [with no] pretension to any great polish or beauty. His illustrations are strik[ing and] well calculated to produce a lasting impression, and, allowing that lib[erty to] others which we claim to ourself, we regard the tone of doctrine a[s ex]cept as sound and Churchman-like."—*Churchman.*

"Of type and paper grateful to the eye, and executed altogeth[er in a] style in which we should like to see all sermons published that are [worth] publishing, which these certainly are. They are plain, straightfo[rward,] instructive, and by no means dry. The writer is unaffectedly in earn[est,] continuing his discourse because he has something to say, and stop[ping] when he is done."—*Evangelical Catholic.*

"Their most marked features are, great simplicity of arrangement, the earnestness and directness with which the preacher ever addresses [him]self to the spiritual wants of his hearers. The Sermons are sixty [in] number, covering a complete Christian year. They embrace a great [va]r[iety] of subjects and are all short. In style, they have the appearance of hav[ing] been written to be preached for the alone object of doing good. Ther[e is] almost nothing in them of doctrinal polemics, but everywhere is seen [the] preacher's great object to reach the hearts and influence the lives of [his] hearers. The circulation of these Sermons cannot but tend to pro[mote] what the Church mainly needs, a living, earnest piety; the noblest [end at] which the Christian minister's ambition can possibly aim."—*Church Re[view.]*

"A volume of Sermons, the genuine fruit of faithful pastoral labor, full of impressive practical views of Christian life and duty. Though [in]tended primarily for Episcopalians, it is adapted to the spiritual wan[ts of] Christians of all communions."—*Christian (Baptist) Review.*

RECENTLY PUBLISHED.

CONFESSION OF CHRIST.

By the same author. Stanford & Swords, 137 Broadway. Price 87½ cts. Desi[gned] as a Manual of preparation for candidates for Baptism, Confirmation, and the L[ord's] Supper.

www.ingramcontent.com/pod-product-compliance
Lightning Source LLC
LaVergne TN
LVHW011139110826
845150LV00008B/2404

* 9 7 8 1 4 1 8 1 9 3 4 6 1 *